WHAT'S WRONG HERE?

AT THE MOVIES

By

Tony Tallarico

Incorporated

Copyright © 1991 Kidsbooks Inc. and Tony Tallarico
7004 N. California Ave.
Chicago, IL. 60645

ANSWERS ON LAST PAGE

It's movie time! Let's all go see our favorite flick! But first, find at least 12 things that are wrong with this picture.

The time is 1849. The place is the American West. The movie studio has spent $100,000,000 to make this film as accurate as possible. However, <u>eleven</u> wrong things have slipped past the director. Can you find them?

Captain Zipp matches his super powers with "The Gang That Couldn't Do Right." What's wrong here? At least <u>12</u> things.

The Ninjas are getting ready to do battle on the big screen...and you are seeing it! Can you also see <u>ten</u> things that are wrong with this picture?

The great detective, Shereluck Homes, is featured in his 249th movie. The old boy is searching for that famous criminal, Professor Moranutty. What he should be searching for is all the things that are wrong in this picture. How many can you find?

SHERELUCK IS AT HIS BEST!

HE WENT TO SCHOOL WITH MY GRAND-FATHER!

Hurry up and sit down! The monster movie has begun. But before you are too comfortably settled in your seat, take a good look and find what's wrong here. Exactly 13 things.

"Grunt!" The movie everyone has been waiting for is now playing at your favorite theater. It's about the world's longest marathon. There are at least 13 things wrong with this race for you to find.

In this movie, Robin Hood and Little John are fighting over the right to cross the log bridge first. Look for and find at least 15 things wrong with this picture.